Ravs

Rays
Short Reflections on Living God's Will

Compiled and with a Foreword
by
Bill Hartnett

NEW CITY PRESS
www.newcitypress.com

Published in the United States by New City Press
202 Comforter Blvd., Hyde Park, NY 12538
www.newcitypress.com
©2011 New City Press

Cover design by Leandro de Leon

Library of Congress Cataloging-in-Publication Data:

Lubich, Chiara, 1920-2008.
  [Selections. English. 2011]
  Rays : short reflections on living God's will / compiled and with a
foreword by Bill Hartnett.
       p. cm.
  Includes bibliographical references (p.   ).
  ISBN 978-1-56548-382-8 (pbk. : alk. paper)
  1. God—Will. 2. Christian life—Catholic authors. I. Hartnett, Bill.
II. Title.
  BT135.L7813 2011
  248.4'82—dc22   2010040707

Printed in the United States of America

Contents

Foreword

*O*nce, while reflecting on God's love in the act of creation, Chiara Lubich used a beautiful metaphor. She spoke of God the Father as an infinite sun, burning with the fire and light and warmth of divine love. And from everywhere inside this infinite sphere only a single word could be heard: Love! Then this word went out from the lips of the Father in the form of a ray. When the ray reached the Son who is the Word, it divided into many rays, each of them the same Love but distinct one from the other, each of them a word in the Word, and creation happened. Each ray became something in creation. One of those rays is you. It was Love, the personal love that rose from the heart of the Father when he thought of you and created you. Chiara describes how each ray continues, on and on, reaching every man, woman, and child on earth no matter where they might be, in whatever time or place, or situation, bringing them the Father's Love and allowing the Father to reach them.

This book is about these rays. Each of us has a ray that burst forth from the Father's heart when he spoke our name with the word Love. If we follow this ray, which is his will for us, what he lovingly desired, and continues in each moment to desire for us, we will become what we are in the mind of God from all eternity. It's a matter of corresponding to his will, adhering to it, moment by moment, until the day when it will literally lead us back to the sun, to the Father. For Chiara, since this ray is Love, then this will of God also leads to our divinization, which is the destiny of every person.

Chiara notes how the rays draw nearer and nearer to each other until they become one in the sun. As we do the will of God, we will become closer and closer to each other, until we are all one in the sun, in God. For Chiara, unity is always the goal, unity as it is found and lived in God who is Love and therefore Trinity. Doing the will of God, therefore, is not a mere individual quest for holiness or perfection. It may indeed lead us to reach Christian perfection as individuals, but its ultimate purpose and consequence is to lead us into the Trinitarian life of communion with God and with our brothers and sisters.

For Chiara, the will of God is not a burdensome task imposed under threat of punishment by some tyrant, as happens with some human masters; rather, it is always an expression of what God's love desires for us. Doing the will of God, therefore, is nothing but responding with our own love to what the Father wishes for us. This was the life of Jesus, who lived the Father's will all the way to the Cross where he cried out the abandonment and, in that agonizing moment, "accomplished" the Father's will by redeeming us. For us too we may have to suffer while carrying out the Father's will, maybe even die, but just as for Jesus, the Resurrection follows. It is the will of the Father that we *live*, Chiara reminds us, and that we experience already here on earth, even amid our sufferings, a joyful foretaste of that new Life that we will share together forever in Heaven. Only after having spent our life on earth in the will of God will we experience the fullness of Life in Heaven where we will finally be realized and fulfilled. This is the mistake that many moderns make, Chiara suggests; having lost sight of Heaven as their goal, they seek fulfillment in material things such as wealth, entertainment, prestige, careers, self-improvement, and knowledge; whereas the most intelligent thing anyone could do is the will of God.

For Chiara, Mary is the prototype of women, for as a woman and especially a Mother, she shares in the greatest charism, the only one that remains in the next life, the one that is the very essence of God himself: Love. For Chiara, Mary is the Woman of Love, the Mother of Fair Love, who spent her entire existence saying yes to Love and being its living *explanation*. But she is also the prototype of every human being. Mary is the person totally open to God and to God's will. She was so transparent that God could look upon her "in her humble state" and see her in the truth, for who she was. Hence, she was drawn into the life of the Holy Trinity and, through the power of the Holy Spirit, became the Mother of Jesus, Mother of God.

In the *Magnificat*, Mary sings of the plan of God being fulfilled in her and through her. With the clarity of vision given to the pure in heart she can see God's divine plan from its beginnings all the way into the future. We too, once we put our lives on course with God's will, often discover that "golden thread" as

Chiara calls it, that presence of God's providential love that runs through the events of our lives and gives new meaning to our past, present and future, bringing healing and wellness and salvation.

Mary gave only one reply to the will of God, "Yes," all the way to the foot of the Cross where she was intimately united with her Son and was mandated by him to be Mother of every believer. This all happened because she always said a sincere and complete "yes" to the will of God. The same can be true for us. If we sincerely open ourselves to the will of God, we discover who we truly are and God — Father, Son, and Spirit — is able to draw us into a deep relationship with the Trinity and transform our lives into a masterpiece of grace for us and for others. In this relationship with the Three, we will also find Mary there; we will discover her as our friend, our partner on the journey, our model, and our Mother.

Bill Hartnett

Short Reflections on Living God's Will

Jesus doesn't care about our
    weaknesses,
our sins,
and our limitations.
He chooses us just as we are.[1]

～

"For he has looked upon the humble
state of his servant" (Lk 1:48–49).
God sees us as we are.[2]

～

Jesus' love will transform us
and give us the strength
    to answer his call.[3]

God calls us to be with him
because he wants to build a personal
relationship with us,
and he invites us
to collaborate with him
in his great plan for humankind.[4]

~

Let us learn to listen
    to the voice of God
deep within our hearts,
which also speaks to us
through the voice of our conscience.[5]

~

God will tell us what he wants from us
in every moment,
and, on our part,
we'll sacrifice everything
in order to do it.[6]

$\mathcal{L}$et us love you, O God,
not only more each day,
for the days that remain may be few,
but let us love you in every present
   moment
with all our heart, soul, and strength
in whatever is your will.
This is the best way to *follow* Jesus.[7]

$\sim$

$\mathcal{O}$f all the commandments in the
   Scriptures,
which one is the most important?
Jesus answers in an unusual way
by joining love of God and love of
   neighbor.
We are never to separate these two loves,
just as we cannot separate the roots of a
tree from its foliage.[8]

"*L*ove the Lord your God with all your heart and with all your soul and with all your mind" (Mt 22:36–37).
Jesus knows that we must truly love God more than anyone else,
and he knows how we should love him:
He is … his God and our God.
He is *my* God and *your* God.
Love the Lord *your* God.[9]

~

*F*or Jesus, loving meant doing the will of the Father,
putting at his Father's disposal his mind, his heart, all his strength,
and even his very life.[10]

*L*oving means doing the will
   of the Beloved,
without half measures,
   with our entire being
— *with all your heart, all your soul
   and all your mind*.
Because love isn't just a matter of feelings.
"Why do you call me, 'Lord, Lord,' but
not do what I command?" (Lk 6:46).[11]

~

Our attitude toward God
should be that of Jesus:
always being turned toward the Father,
listening to him,
in obedience,
in order to carry out his work —
that alone and nothing else.[12]

We cannot give less than
   everything to God:
all our heart, all our soul, all our mind.
And this means doing completely and well
whatever he asks of us.[13]

~

Yes, my God,
in this moment,
in this action,
I love you....
This is the only way that we can reciprocate
his being Love for us.[14]

~

What must we do?
Renew our choice of God.
Give him first place and live his will
perfectly in the present moment.
We want to be able to say:
"I love you, I'm all yours, you are my
God, our God of infinite Love!"[15]

"My food is to do the will of the one who sent me,
and to complete his work" (Jn 4:34).
These wondrous words of Jesus
     can be repeated,
by every Christian and,
if put into practice,
they are capable of carrying us far on the journey of life.[16]

~

Jesus came down from heaven
to do the will of the one who sent him and to finish his work (see Jn 4:34).
He didn't have thoughts or an agenda
     of his own,
but only those of his Father.[17]

The words Jesus spoke
and the works he did
were those of the Father;
he didn't do his own will.
This was the life of Jesus.[18]

~

Complete adherence to the Father's will
was the characteristic of Jesus' whole life,
all the way to his death on the cross,
where he truly completed the work
that the Father had entrusted to him.[19]

~

Jesus considered the will of the Father
as his food,
because by doing it,
"assimilating" it,
"eating" it,
identifying with it,
he received Life.[20]

And what was the will of the Father, his work that Jesus had to finish?
It was to give salvation to all people, to give them the Life that doesn't die.[21]

～

In speaking to a Samaritan woman
(see Jn 4:4–29),
Jesus revealed the plan of God
    who is a Father:
that all people receive the gift of Life.
This is the work that Jesus earnestly wanted to finish.[22]

～

We should live as sons and daughters of the Father
by living the Life that Jesus shared with us,
then our lives will be nourished
    on his will.[23]

By saying yes to God
— and not to herself —
Mary became Mother of God.[24]

～

"My food is to do the will of the one
who sent me" (Jn 4:34).
Let us feed on what God wants from us
moment by moment
and we'll find that it satisfies us:
it gives us peace, joy, happiness.
It will give us
a foretaste of Heaven.[25]

～

Jesus teaches us
that the Father has a plan of love for each
one of us,
that he loves us personally
and that if we believe in his love
and respond with our love,
he directs all things toward good.[26]

For Jesus,
nothing happens by chance,
not even his passion and death.
And this was followed by his
Resurrection.[27]

~

The example of the Risen Jesus
should be a source of light for our lives.
We should learn how to see everything
that happens to us,
everything around us
and even everything that makes us suffer
as something that God wills or permits
because he loves us.[28]

"Not what I will but what you will"
(Mk 14:36).
Then everything will find a meaning in
our lives;
everything will be extremely useful,
even what might seem to be
    incomprehensible and absurd,
even what might plunge us into mortal
anguish,
as happened to Jesus.[29]

≈

With him we need only repeat,
with total trust in the Father's love:
"Not what I will but what you will"
(Mk 14:36).[30]

His will is not,
as we might sometimes think,
a burden that we have
     to resign ourselves to;
nor is it a monotonous task allotted to us
during our lifetime.
His will is that we *live*
and that we joyfully thank him
for the gifts we've received.[31]

~

The will of God.
Here is a way to holiness
wide open to every human being.[32]

God's will is like the sun
whose rays are like his will
    for each one of us.
Each of us walks along a ray,
distinct from the ray
    of the person next to us,
but always along a ray of the sun,
that is, the will of God.[33]

~

The closer the rays get to the sun,
the closer they get to each other.
For us too, the closer we come to God,
by carrying out the divine will,
    more and more,
the closer we draw to each other …
until we are *all one*.[34]

~

We can cooperate with Jesus,
day by day,
in finishing the work of the Father. [35]

By living the will of God,
everything changes in our life.
Instead of seeking people we like
and loving only them,
we reach out to all those
the will of God puts next to us.[36]

~

The will of God
is his Voice
that continually speaks to us
and invites us.
It's the way in which he expresses
    his love
in order to give us the fullness
    of his Life.[37]

"Not what I will, but what you will"
(Mk 14:36).
Being intent on what God wants
    in each moment
(*what you will*)
detaches us from everything else,
and from ourselves
(*not what I will*).[38]

~

Detachment is not something we
deliberately strive for
— we seek God —
but we do attain it.
Then our joy is complete.
And all we have to do is immerse
    ourselves in each fleeting moment
and, in that moment,
carry out the will of God.[39]

Just as someone traveling by train
would never go walking
    up and down the aisle
in order to reach his destination sooner,
but remain seated,
so we should remain in the present.
The train of time moves forward
    on its own.
We can love God only
    in the present moment. [40]

~

We can only love God
    in the present moment.
Let us love, therefore,
by giving that smile,
by doing that job,
by driving that car,
by cooking that meal,
by organizing that activity
    for someone in need. [41]

Trials and sufferings need not frighten
us if,
with Jesus,
we know how to recognize God's will in
them, that is:
his *love* for each one of us.[42]

~

Lord, help me not to fear anything,
for all that will happen
Will simply be *your will!*
Lord, help me not to desire anything,
for nothing is more desirable
    than *your will*.
What matters in life?
What matters is *your will*.
Grant that nothing may disturb me,
for in everything is *your will*.
Grant that nothing swells my pride,
For all is *your will*.[43]

"May it be done to me according to
your word" (Lk 1:38).
Since Mary carried out not her own will
but the will of God,
since she trusted in God unconditionally,
all generations have called her blessed
(see Lk 1:48).
She fulfilled herself completely
and became the woman *par excellence*.[44]

∾

This is the fruit of doing God's will:
we acquire total freedom,
and we become our true self.[45]

∾

God has always thought of us,
he's loved us from all eternity;
we've always had a place in his heart.[46]

God wants to reveal to each of us,
as he did to Mary,
our true identity.[47]

~

God seems to ask:
"Would you like me to make a masterpiece
of you and your life?"
Then follow the way I show you
and you will become what you always are
in my heart."[48]

~

By telling you his will,
God is revealing to you
your true self.[49]

His will is the expression
  of his love for us,
of his plan for us
and so it is sublime as God himself,
deeply fascinating
and enchanting
as is his countenance.[50]

~

We too,
like Mary,
are called to say:
"Behold, I am the servant of the Lord.
May it be done to me according
  to your word"
(Lk 1:38).

The will of God
is the best,
the most intelligent thing
we can do.[51]

$\mathcal{M}$ary, who, like every Jewish girl,
pondered in her heart,
who would be the Mother of the Messiah,
teaches us something:
By inserting herself into what
   God was thinking,
she accomplished in her life what she had
always dreamed of
and even more.[52]

~

$\mathcal{M}$ary's words: "Behold I am the
servant of the Lord,"
could be our response of love
to the Love of God.[53]

No event,
be it joyful,
indifferent,
or sad,
is without meaning.
Everything contributes to the fulfillment
of God's plan
which we discover, day by day,
doing the will of God
as Mary did.[54]

~

Let us say it before every action:
"May it be done. May your will be
done."
Then, moment by moment,
piece by piece,
we will be crafting the wondrous,
unique, and unrepeatable
mosaic of our life that the Lord had in
mind for each one of us.[55]

Let's decide
to know his will
as it is expressed in his Word.[56]

~

Jesus manifests himself
to those who love him
by putting his commandments into
practice (see Jn 14:21).[57]

~

Although states in life
are some more and others less perfect,
perfection can be attained
only by doing the will of God.[58]

~

To reach holiness,
it's enough to do
his will.[59]

The will of God.
What a wondrous discovery!
And practical too!
Here's a way of holiness that's perfect
    for everyone:
men and women,
young and old,
gifted and less gifted,
intellectuals and laborers,
mothers and those in religious life,
lay people and clergy,
government officials and ordinary citizens.[60]

~

The will of God means having
    in your hands
the passport to perfection —
not only for an elite group of persons
called to priesthood or to religious life,
but for the masses.[61]

What?
Resign ourselves to God's will?
On the contrary!
We should have to resign ourselves
if we do our own dull will,
so unprofitable and inconclusive![62]

~

We should *want* to do God's will
because it is the greatest thing
   we could desire.
And we shouldn't say,
   "I *must* do God's will,"
but rather, "I *can* do God's will!"[63]

~

Two roads lie before us in life and,
like everybody else,
we have to choose between them:
We can spend this life
following our own will
or following God's will.[64]

Complete trust in God
doesn't mean we become passive.
Quite the contrary:
once we grasp God's will,
we make it our own and carry it out with
all our heart, soul, and strength,
staying faithful to it even though it's
constantly changing.[65]

~

We know that God's will
is a Father's will.[66]

~

We can place ourselves
in God's hands
without fear.[67]

~

Anything he wills
will be for our good.[68]

Before long,
we acquire a considerable amount of
flexibility one must have
in order to be able to understand his will.[69]

~

Every circumstance is
an expression of his love for us.[70]

~

When we don't know what God wants,
we do what we think best,
asking God to put us back
   on the right track
if we've made the wrong choice.[71]

~

By living this way
we are putting into effect a divine plan,
about which we know nothing
except that we are being guided by God,
our Father.[72]

Jesus was our example.
We imitated him, not in an exterior way,
but in the fact
that, like him,
we wanted to do God's will.[73]

~

When we have succeeded in being
able to be like Christ
in his determined and total obedience
   to the Father,
then we will experience inner unity.[74]

~

We must not imitate the saints by
mindlessly copying their actions,
but by striving to do God's will
   as they had done.[75]

How different the saints were from
each other;
yet they were identical in one thing:
they had all done God's will.[76]

~

Being consecrated to God
with vows is important,
but God's will is more important.[77]

~

You get married,
and you do God's will.
I live a life of virginity.
But we are equal
because what is important is God's will.[78]

God's will is what binds us together
as one family
with Jesus our brother
and God our Father (see Mk 3:31–35).[79]

~

We've chosen God and,
in order to be faithful to this choice,
we must put into practice
     the commandment
that Jesus calls *his own*:
"My command is this: Love each other
as I have loved you" (Jn 15:12).[80]

~

It is by living the new commandment
that the unity willed by Jesus
will be brought about
and it will enable us to have
     Jesus in our midst.[81]

After Jesus,
Mary is the one
who most perfectly says yes to God.
This is where her holiness lies
and her greatness.[82]

~

God focused our attention
on the new commandment,
and now we realize
that it is the very heart of Christianity.[83]

~

Even civil laws
are an expression of God's will for us.[84]

~

We have a kind of compass
for discerning God's will.
It is the Voice of the Holy Spirit
within us (see Jn 14:15–21). [85]

We often say that we live between
   two "fires":
God within us and God among us.
Here in this divine "furnace"
we are formed and trained
to listen to Jesus
and to follow him.[86]

~

Jesus among us
is like a loud-speaker
that amplifies God's voice
within each one of us,
enabling us to hear it more clearly.[87]

~

In order to understand God's will,
a person should be part of a Christian
community
where Christ is present and alive
(see Phil 1:9–10).[88]

The only *time* in our possession
is the present moment.[89]

∼

The past no longer exists;
let's entrust it to God's mercy.[90]

∼

By living the present,
we will also live the future well
when it becomes present.[91]

∼

Those who are more inclined to carry
out the expressed will of God,
tend not to notice when circumstances
indicate a new course of God's will
and consequently they tend to have a less
intimate relationship with him,
not giving themselves to him with all
their heart.[92]

The most beautiful characteristic
of the Gospel
is the *normality* of a life that is supernatu-
ral but simple;
neither artificial nor excessive,
but pure and harmonious — like nature,
like Mary.[93]

∼

Each one of us does the will of the
Father
and this binds us to each other,
to Jesus, and to the Father.[94]

∼

The rays of the sun are *one* with the sun.
Similarly, God's will coincides with God.
by loving his will, we are loving him.[95]

When we succeed in doing his will,
moment by moment,
we experience that his yoke is easy,
his burden light (see Mt 11:29).

~

Being completely intent on God's will
in each moment
frees us from everything else,
and from ourselves.[96]

~

Previously we used to associate with
people we liked,
those we loved and found pleasant.
Now we are happy to seek the company of
whomever God wills us to be with,
and we would stay with them
for as long as he wills it![97]

Two things cannot occupy our
  attention at the same time.
So rather than laboring to eradicate
  our own will,
we should work at acquiring
  the divine will.[98]

~

If we have not loved God in the
  previous moments,
we at least have to love him
  in the present moment.[99]

~

With each passing moment
of each new day,
we are adding stitches
  to a magnificent embroidery.[100]

Mary was silent
because she was a created being,
and nothingness doesn't speak.
But upon that nothingness
Jesus spoke and said:
Himself.[101]

~

The moments not spent "on our ray"
we entrust to God's mercy.
From our vantage point, from the
    underside of the embroidery,
these moments seem like so many knots
in the threads.
But we are certain that God's love mends
every tear
and binds every broken thread.[102]

~

From heaven
our lives will be seen
    as the wonderful stories
of the children of God.[103]

What about our mistakes,
our weakness?
Catherine of Siena offers us some
    encouraging words:
"All that God wills or permits is for our
sanctification."[104]

~

If we make a mistake
we can't let it discourage us.
Whatever happened,
if entrusted to God's mercy,
will not only cease to be useless or harmful,
but will help us to acquire humility,
the foundation of holiness.[105]

~

Outside God's will
we found no light,
no love,
no peace,
— only torment.[106]

We admire Mary
as the most perfect human being who
ever lived,
because she did only God's will.[107]

∼

If doing God's will means to live
   like Jesus,
it also means to live like Mary.
And this is the best way to show our
devotion to her
and to be her children.
For she says: "I am the servant of the
Lord. Let it be done to me according to
your word" (Lk 1:38).[108]

∼

Since we love him
in doing his will,
he manifests himself to us.
"I will manifest myself to the one who
loves me" (see Jn 14:21).[109]

By living God's will
we become more united
not only with God
but also with each other.
And so we are transformed
both personally
and collectively
into Christ.[110]

~

... "On earth as in heaven."
And what is the will of God
that we will do forever in heaven?
We will live in communion,
a communion of Love.[111]

~

We cannot but take inspiration
from Mary
in her desire to do the will of God.[112]

God
sees and knows
the course we must follow
every instant of our lives.[113]

~

For each of us
He has established a celestial orbit
in which the star of our freedom
ought to turn
if it abandons itself
to the One who created it.[114]

~

The voice of God,
which is his will,
speaks clearly
in Mary's soul,
because she listens.[115]

*O*ur life
does not collide
with the orbits of our brothers
    and sisters,
children of the Father like us,
but harmonizes with them
in a firmament
more splendid than the stars,
because it is spiritual.[116]

~

*H*e is Father,
Love.
He is Creator,
Redeemer,
Sanctifier.
Who better than he knows
what is good for us?[117]

The will of God
is deep as God himself.
It's divine and
sublime as his Love.[118]

≈

The will of God
is the voice of God
which continually calls
and invites us.[119]

≈

The will of God
is a golden thread
which weaves together
our earthly life
and beyond.[120]

The will of God
is God's way
of expressing
his love,
love that calls for a response,
so that he can accomplish
wonderful things
in us.[121]

≈

It is precisely in living
what he has in mind for us
that our personalities
are developed.[122]

≈

We set up goals
to reach,
not realizing that the history of the world
and of each individual
are in *his* hands.[123]

*O*n earth
Jesus saw
neither the initial expansion of the Church
nor its later achievements.
Yet, he said that he had completed
his work.[124]

≈

*I*f God's will is first and foremost for me,
if it reigns over everything else,
even over those things
I can and should love,
then God is truly the Ruler
of my heart.[125]

≈

*I*f I allow
other things,
persons, or ideas
to reign in me,
then God is like a king dethroned
    from my heart
by my ego.[126]

I can be like Mary.
Moment by moment
I can offer myself to the Light.
And the Spirit in me will say
(as when he burst forth from the heart
    of our Mother):
"My soul praises the Lord!" (Lk 1:46).[127]

～

Sometimes you could think that
    to love God,
some verbal expressions are sufficient
or that it's a matter of feeling it.
No: Loving God means doing his will.[128]

～

Not doing our will but his means:
not programming for our own lives
things that are limiting and unsatisfying
because they come from our own mind;
but rather, to abandon ourselves to the plan
that God in his love,
has for each one of us.[129]

Nowadays,
people's plans are:
to find a good job,
to be financially taken care of,
to hold a good position in society.
Work is seen as a way to be better off,
having a second house,
a second car, the latest communication
devices, etc. Free time is geared toward
having new experiences,
getting to know new things,
enjoyment and pleasure.
Travelling is all the rage, tourism, and
entertainment, seeing shows.
These are the plans of people who don't know
what they could experience on earth
if they lived as the sons and daughters of God.[130]

When we do the will of God,
the Lord responds to our love
with his Love.[131]

~

There is one will of God,
described in a commandment of Jesus,
the one about love of neighbor.
It's extremely important because,
at the end of our lives,
we'll be judged on it.[132]

~

Mary is the most perfect human being
that ever lived on earth,
for she only did the will of God.[133]

"The Father is greater than I am"
(Jn 14:12).
The entire universe is a living Gospel
and each lower creature serves the one
above it.
Each thing in nature acquires importance
inasmuch as it relates to the superior one.
And so every human being has to lose
himself in *God*
in order to "become" God.
He has to be *pure will of God*
in order to be the expression of God,
of God's love
here below. [134]

"*My* food is to do the will of my Father."
Jesus was nothing but the living will
    of the Father;
they were a single will,
for Jesus used his human and divine will
to do the will of the Father.
And he denied his own will: "… your will
be done" (Mk 14:36).
He loved himself only in relation
    to the Father.[135]

~

"*Not* my will but yours be done"
(Mt 26:39).
Ah! The will of God!
The will of God! It made St. Mary
Magdalen de' Pazzi
go into ecstasy at the mere mention
    of the words!
Today, I'll do the will of God, I'll deny
myself in the will of God,
I'll surrender to the will of God.[136]

Notes

[1] Word of Life, *Living City* 44/6 (June 2005).

[2] Word of Life, *Living City* 41/12 (December 2002).

[3] Word of Life, *Living City* 44/6 (June 2005).

[4] Ibid.

[5] Ibid.

[6] Ibid.

[7] Ibid.

[8] Word of Life, *Living City* 41/10 (October 2002).

[9] Ibid.

[10] Ibid.

[11] Ibid.

[12] Ibid.

[13] Ibid.

[14] Ibid.

[15] Ibid.

[16] Ibid.

[17] Ibid.

[18] Ibid.

[19] Ibid.

[20] Ibid.

[21] Ibid.

[22] Ibid.

[23] Ibid.

[24] Maria Leonor Salierno, *Maria negli scritti di Chiara Lubich* (Rome: Città Nuova Editrice, 1994), p. 143.

[25] Word of Life, *Living City* 41/10 (October 2002).

[26] Ibid.

[27] Ibid.

[28] Ibid.

[29] Ibid.

[30] Ibid.

[31] Ibid.

[32] Chiara Lubich, *A Call to Love* (New York: New City Press, 1989), pp. 25–38.

[33] Word of Life, *Living City* 41/10 (October 2002).

[34] Ibid.

[35] Ibid.

[36] Ibid.

[37] Ibid.

[38] Ibid.

[39] Ibid.

[40] Ibid.

[41] Ibid.

[42] Ibid.

[43] Ibid.

[44] Ibid.

[45] Ibid.

[46] Ibid.

[47] Ibid.

[48] Ibid.

[49] Ibid.

[50] Word of Life, *Living City* 41/10 (October 2002).

51 Ibid.

52 Maria Leonor Salierno, *Maria negli scritti di Chiara Lubich* (Rome: Città Nuova Editrice, 1994), p. 143.

53 Word of Life, *Living City* 41/12 (December 2002).

54 Ibid.

55 Ibid.

56 Word of Life, *Living City* 32/8–9 (August/September 1993).

57 Ibid.

58 Ibid.

59 Chiara Lubich, *A Call to Love* (New York: New City Press, 1989), pp. 25-38.

60 Ibid.

61 Ibid.

62 Ibid.

63 Ibid.

64 Ibid.

65 Ibid.

66 Ibid.

67 Ibid.

68 Ibid.

69 Ibid.

70 Ibid.

71 Ibid.

72 Ibid.

73 Ibid.

74 Ibid.

75 Ibid.

76 Ibid.

77 Ibid.

78 Ibid.

79 Ibid.

80 Ibid.

81 Ibid.

82 Maria Leonor Salierno, *Maria negli scritti di Chiara Lubich* (Rome: Città Nuova Editrice, 1994), p. 143.

83 Chiara Lubich, *A Call to Love* (New York: New City Press, 1989), pp. 25–38.

84 Ibid.

85 Ibid.

86 Ibid.

87 Ibid.

88 Ibid.

89 Ibid.

90 Ibid.

91 Ibid.

92 Ibid.

93 Ibid.

94 Ibid.

95 Ibid.

96 Ibid.

97 Ibid.

98 Ibid.

99 Ibid.

100 Ibid.

101 Maria Leonor Salierno, *Maria negli scritti di Chiara Lubich* (Rome: Città Nuova Editrice, 1994), p. 39.

102 Chiara Lubich, *A Call to Love* (New York: New City Press, 1989), pp. 25–38.

103 Ibid.

104 Ibid.

105 Ibid.

106 Ibid.

107 Ibid.

[108] Ibid.

[109] Ibid.

[110] Ibid.

[111] Chiara Lubich, Writing, 1999.

[112] Maria Leonor Salierno, *Maria negli scritti di Chiara Lubich* (Rome: Città Nuova Editrice, 1994), p. 143.

[113] Chiara Lubich, *L'attrattiva del tempo moderno (Scritti spirituali 1)* (Rome: Città Nuova Editrice, 1977), p. 101 (our translation).

[114] Ibid.

[115] Maria Leonor Salierno, *Maria negli scritti di Chiara Lubich* (Rome: Città Nuova Editrice, 1994), p. 43.

[116] Chiara Lubich, *L'attrattiva del tempo moderno (Scritti spirituali 1)* (Rome: Città Nuova Editrice, 1977), p. 101 (our translation).

[117] Ibid.

[118] Chiara Lubich, *Santi insieme* (Rome: Città Nuova Editrice, 1994), pp. 97–98 (our translation).

[119] Chiara Lubich, *L'attrattiva del tempo moderno (Scritti spirituali 1)* (Rome: Città Nuova Editrice, 1977), p. 101 (our translation).

[120] Chiara Lubich, *Santità di popolo* (Rome: Città Nuova Editrice, 2001), pp. 97–98 (our translation).

[121] Chiara Lubich, *L'attrattiva del tempo moderno (Scritti spirituali 1)* (Rome: Città Nuova Editrice, 1977), p. 101 (our translation).

[122] Ibid.

[123] Chiara Lubich, *L'essenziale di oggi (Scritti spirituali 2)* (Rome: Città Nuova Editrice, 1978), p. 95 (our translation).

[124] Chiara Lubich, *L'attrattiva del tempo moderno (Scritti spirituali 1)* (Rome: Città Nuova Editrice, 1977), p. 101 (our translation).

[125] Chiara Lubich, *L'essenziale di oggi (Scritti spirituali 2)* (Rome: Città Nuova Editrice, 1978), pp. 236–37 (our translation).

[126] Ibid.

[127] Maria Leonor Salierno, *Maria negli scritti di Chiara Lubich* (Rome: Città Nuova Editrice, 1994), p. 34.

[128] Maria Leonor Salierno, *Maria negli scritti di Chiara Lubich* (Rome: Città Nuova Editrice, 1994), p. 190,

[129] Ibid.

[130] Ibid.

[131] Ibid.

[132] Ibid., p. 191.

[133] Ibid., p. 153.

[134] Lubich, Chiara. Writing 1950.

[135] Lubich, Chiara. Writing 1950.

[136] Maria Leonor Salierno, *Maria negli scritti di Chiara Lubich* (Rome: Città Nuova Editrice, 1994), p. 150.

For Further Reading

Chiara Lubich, *Essential Writings: Spirituality, Dialogue, Culture* (Hyde Park, NY: New City Press, 2007), 66–76.

Chiara Lubich, *A New Way: The Spirituality of Unity* (Hyde Park, NY: New City Press, 2006), 41–43.

Chiara Lubich, *Here and Now: Meditations on Living in the Present* (Hyde Park, NY: New City Press, 2000).